Ee

Bela Davis

Abdo
THE ALPHABET
Kids

abdopublishing.com

Published by Abdo Kids, a division of ABDO, PO Box 398166, Minneapolis, Minnesota 55439.
Copyright © 2017 by Abdo Consulting Group, Inc. International copyrights reserved in all countries.
No part of this book may be reproduced in any form without written permission from the publisher.

Printed in the United States of America, North Mankato, Minnesota.

102016

012017

 THIS BOOK CONTAINS
RECYCLED MATERIALS

Photo Credits: Glow Images, iStock, Shutterstock

Production Contributors: Teddy Borth, Jennie Forsberg, Grace Hansen

Design Contributors: Christina Doffing, Candice Keimig, Dorothy Toth

Publisher's Cataloging in Publication Data

Names: Davis, Bela, author.

Title: Ee / by Bela Davis.

Description: Minneapolis, Minnesota : Abdo Kids, 2017 | Series: The alphabet |
    Includes bibliographical references and index.

Identifiers: LCCN 2016943885 | ISBN 9781680808810 (lib. bdg.) |
    ISBN 9781680795912 (ebook) | ISBN 9781680796582 (Read-to-me ebook)

Subjects: LCSH: English language--Alphabet--Juvenile literature. | Alphabet
    books--Juvenile literature.

Classification: DDC 421/.1--dc23

LC record available at http://lccn.loc.gov/2016943885

Table of Contents

Ee

Emma has gr**ee**n **eye**s.

Ee

Erin mad**e** an **eagle**.

Ee

Eric **e**ats an **e**gg.

Ee

Elijah and **E**mily ar**e e**ight.

10

Ee

Elena lik**es** to **exercise**.

13

Ee

Ellie thinks baking is **e**asy.

Ee

Ethan looks at an **eel**.

Ee

Ed wins chess every time.

18

Ee

What is **E**van dr**e**ss**e**d as?

(an **ele**phant)

21

More **Ee** Words

eggplant

elf

elbow

eraser

Glossary

eagle
when a golfer gets the ball in the hole by hitting it two less times than what is expected for it to take.

eel
a long fish that looks like a snake and has smooth slippery skin.

exercise
physical activity that is done in order to get stronger and healthier.

Index

abdokids.com

Use this code to log on to abdokids.com and access crafts, games, videos, and more!

Abdo Kids Code:
TEK8810